Why Why Why did Romans race to the circus?

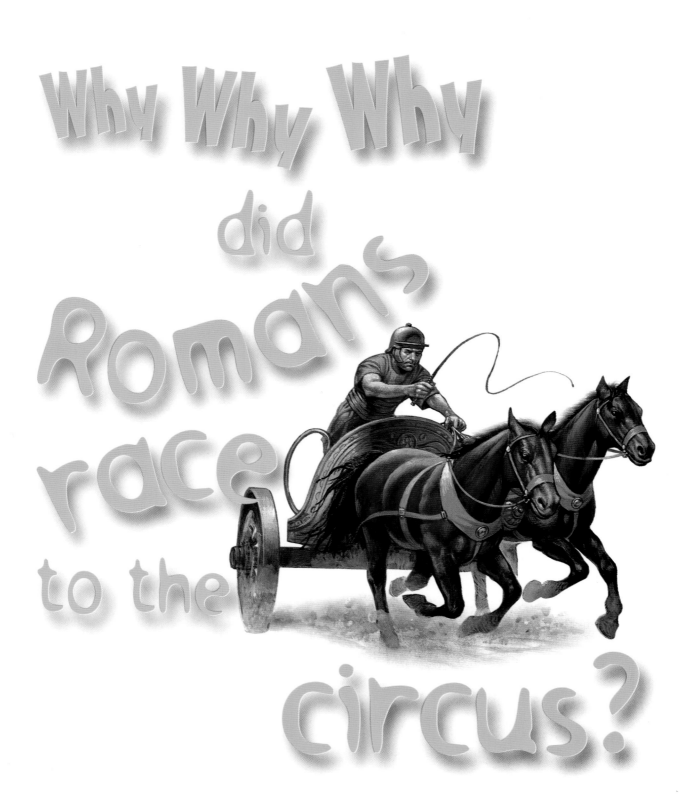

Miles Kelly
PUBLISHING

First published in 2006 by
Miles Kelly Publishing Ltd
Bardfield Centre, Great Bardfield, Essex, CM7 4SL

Copyright © Miles Kelly Publishing Ltd 2006

2 4 6 8 10 9 7 5 3 1

Editorial Director
Belinda Gallagher

Art Director
Jo Brewer

Volume Designer
Michelle Cannatella

Indexer
Susan Bosanko

Production Manager
Elizabeth Brunwin

Reprographics
Anthony Cambray, Mike Coupe, Ian Paulyn

Character Cartoonist
Mike Foster

All other artworks from the Miles Kelly Archives

ISBN 1-84236-703-X

Printed in China

British Library Cataloguing-in-Publication Data
A catalogue record for this book is available
from the British Library

www.mileskelly.net
info@mileskelly.net

Contents

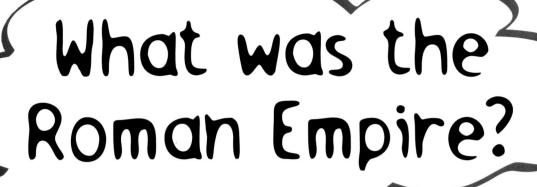

What was the Roman Empire?

Rome is a city in modern-day Italy. About 3000 years ago, it was just a small village. It began to grow into a large, powerful city. About 2000 years ago, Rome ruled many different lands. All of these lands, including Rome itself, were known as the Roman Empire.

Rome

Find out

The Roman Empire was huge. Try to find out which countries were part of it.

4

Where did people go shopping?

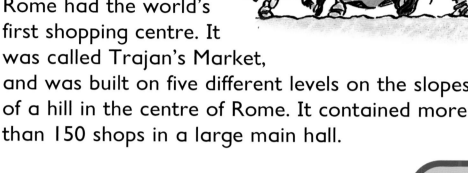

Rome had the world's first shopping centre. It was called Trajan's Market, and was built on five different levels on the slopes of a hill in the centre of Rome. It contained more than 150 shops in a large main hall.

Time to go!

The Romans designed the first public toilets. Users sat next to each other on rows of seats.

Did people live in blocks of flats?

The Romans built the world's first high-rise flats. Most people who lived in Ostia, a busy town close to Rome, lived in blocks of flats known as 'insulae'. Each block had up to 100 small rooms.

Blocks of flats

What did the Romans eat?

Preparing dinner

People ate just bread and fruit for breakfast. Lunch might be leftovers from the night before. The main meal was eaten in the evening. It might include meat such as goose or hare, and vegetables and fruit. It took all day to prepare.

Plan

Find out what the Romans ate then plan your own Roman menu. Include a starter, main dish and dessert.

Did people have dinner parties?

Yes, they did – and they lay down to eat! People lay on long couches around a table. They often wore crowns of flowers and they took off their sandals before entering the dining room.

Dinner party

Yuk!
Yummy dishes for a Roman banquet might include eel, thrush, dormouse or poached snails. If that upset people's stomachs, pickled cabbage was eaten to make them feel better!

Who ate takeaways?

Ordinary people did. Many went to cheap eating houses for their main meal, or bought ready-cooked snacks from roadside fast-food stalls.

What did children learn at school?

Only boys went to school. At the age of six they began to learn reading, writing, arithmetic, history and sport. They were also taught public speaking.

At school →

Inky fingers!

Soot from wood fires was used to make ink. It was mixed with vinegar and sticky gum that oozed from trees. Some Roman writing has survived 2000 years.

Did children use calculators?

Calculators hadn't been invented, so children learned to count with their fingers! A wooden counting frame called an abacus was used to work out sums.

Count

If boys started school aged 6 and left when they were 16, how many years did they study for?

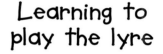
Learning to play the lyre

Why didn't girls go to school?

Roman girls were expected to stay at home and learn how to run a household. This was training for when they were married. Most girls were taught how to play a musical instrument called the lyre.

What was a toga?

Toga

Most men wore a long robe called a toga. It looked good, but it was bulky and uncomfortable to wear. Important men wore togas with a purple trim. Most children wore togas, too. Married ladies wore a dress called a 'stola' and a shawl called a 'palla' over the top of it.

Did people wear make-up?

Both men and women wore make-up. The Romans admired pale, smooth skin. Crushed chalk was used as face powder, red ochre (crumbly earth) for blusher and plant juice for lipstick.

Palla

Stola

'Scare' cut!
Going to the barbers could be very painful. Scissors and razors had not been invented. Barbers used big, sharp shears to trim men's hair and beards!

Hairstyles

Find out
What did Julius Caesar wear on his head?

What were Roman hairstyles like?

Hairstyles went in and out of fashion. Women would curl, plait or pin up their hair. Wigs and hair extensions were popular, as were headdresses and hairbands.

Who wore precious jewels?

Men and women wore rings of gold, silver or bronze. Many of these rings were decorated with amber or precious stones. Rich ladies wore necklaces and earrings of gold and pearls, while poorer women made do with beads of glass or ceramics. Cloaks were fastened with fine brooches.

Necklace

Ring

Baby love!

Romans gave a good luck charm called a 'bulla' to their babies to keep them safe from harm.

Earrings

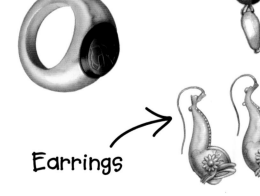

What was a mosaic?

The Romans liked their homes to look good, too. Beautiful pictures called mosaics decorated floors. Each mosaic was made from thousands of small tiles made from coloured stone or pottery.

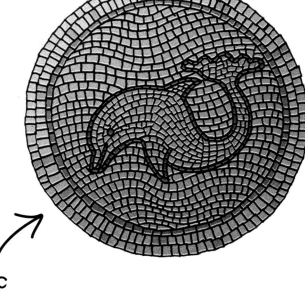

Mosaic

Make

Look at some Roman mosaics in a book then make your own using squares of coloured card.

Did people wear shoes?

Most people wore leather sandals. Soldiers wore these too, but with studded soles so they were not worn out by marching. Boots were worn for riding.

How clean were the Romans?

The Romans were very clean. They often visited the public baths. These huge buildings were also fitness centres and a place to meet friends. Visitors could take part in sports, such as wrestling, have a massage or even get their hair cut.

Cool bath

Cold bath

Fire to heat water

What a stink!

Although the Romans liked bathing, they only visited the baths once in every nine days.

Did the Romans listen to music?

The Romans liked music and dancing. Ordinary people liked listening to pipes, flutes, cymbals and horns. Rich people preferred the quieter sound of the lyre.

Roman bath house

Hot bath

Board game

Think

Roman baths were a good place for people to meet their friends. Think about where you go to meet your friends.

What games did people play?

Popular Roman games were 'Tables', 'Robbers' and 'Three Stones' — a version of noughts-and-crosses. A favourite girls' game was tossing little bones into the air and seeing how many they could catch on the back of the hand.

What was the Colosseum?

The Colosseum was an amazing building. It was a huge oval arena in the centre of Rome, used for fights between men called gladiators, and for pretend sea battles. Up to 50,000 people could sit inside. It was built of stone, concrete and marble and had 80 entrances.

The Colosseum

Draw

Romans followed chariot racing like we support football. Draw a poster advertising a chariot race.

Did Romans race to the circus?

The Romans liked a day at the races. Horses pulled chariots around a track, called a 'circus'. The most famous was Circus Maximus. Twelve chariots took part in each race, running seven times round the track.

Chariot racing

Superstars!
Some gladiators became so popular that people wrote graffiti about them on walls.

Was chariot racing dangerous?

Yes it was. Chariots often smashed into each other and overturned. Each driver carried a sharp knife called a 'falx', to cut himself free if this happened. Many horses and drivers were killed.

What was army life like?

Roman soldiers were well paid and well cared for. They were often called upon to defend the Roman Empire from enemies, so the army was very important. Soldiers were trained in battle and often had to march long distances along straight roads.

Brrrr!

Roman soldiers guarding the cold northern frontiers of Britain kept warm by wearing short woollen trousers, like underpants, beneath their tunics!

Testudo

Was a tortoise used in battle?

When soldiers had to defend themselves against enemy attack, they used a 'tortoise'. Their shields made a protective 'shell' around them. It was called a 'testudo', or tortoise. Soldiers carried three main weapons – javelins, swords and daggers.

Did soldiers cook dinner?

Yes they did. Soldiers had to find or make everything they needed to survive. They built camps and forts defended by walls. Soldiers had to be able to cook, build, and be doctors, blacksmiths and engineers – and they all had to fight!

Roman soldiers

Discover

Can you find out which famous British queen the Romans had trouble defeating?

What was a villa?

Villas were large Roman country houses. They were surrounded by orchards, fields, flocks of sheep or herds of cattle. Country villas were owned mainly by the rich. The first villas were small farmhouses, but as Rome became powerful, villas became magnificent mansions.

Pets

Roman villa

Garden

Plan

Plan your own villa. Draw pictures of how it might look.

Did people keep pets?

Roman families liked to keep pets. Statues and paintings show many children playing with their pets. Dogs, cats and doves were all popular. Some families also kept ornamental fish and tame deer.

Love struck!

The Romans invented Valentine's Day, but called it 'Lupercalia'. Boys picked a girl's name from a hat, and she was meant to be their girlfriend for the year!

Bedroom

Kitchen

Where did people go on holiday?

In the summer, Rome became hot, stuffy, smelly and dirty. Rich Romans often had two homes, so they would leave the city and escape to their villa in the countryside.

Why were farms important?

In Roman times, most people lived and worked on farms. Without farms, the people of Rome would starve. Farmers produced food for city people, which was grown on big estates by teams of slaves, and on small peasant farms where single families worked together.

Squeaky clean!

When Romans bathed, they covered their bodies in olive oil and then scraped it off to remove all the dirt and sweat!

Farm

Olives

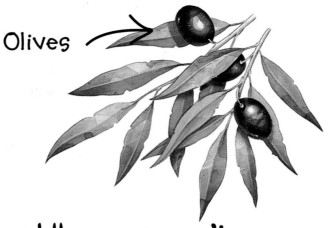

Why were olives so special?

Olives grow on trees. The Romans used them as food, or crushed them to make oil. Olive oil was used as medicine, in cooking, for cleansing the skin — and even for burning in lamps.

Imagine

Imagine you are a Roman farm worker, what job would you do and why?

Did grapes grow on trees?

Roman grapes did grow on trees, almost! Vines are climbing plants that produce grapes. The Romans planted them among fruit trees, which supported the vines as they grew.

Who was the top god?

The Romans worshipped many different gods. Jupiter was king of the gods. His wife Juno was worshipped by married women. Mars was the god of war and Venus was the goddess of love. Neptune, god of the sea, sent earthquakes and terrible storms. Messenger of the gods was Mercury.

Jupiter and Juno

Mars and Venus

Neptune

Find out

School children had their own goddess. Can you find out what she was called? Use a book to help you.

Did people go to church?

Temples were beautiful buildings. They were built so that people could worship the gods. At the centre was a shrine. Here, people would leave food and wine as gifts to the gods.

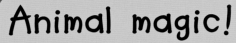

Temple

Which god started storms?

Neptune was god of the sea. The Romans believed he could start and stop storms. He was also the god of earthquakes. Sea travel was dangerous in Roman times, so sailors prayed to Neptune to keep them safe on their journeys.

Mercury

Why were roads always straight?

The Romans built thousands of kilometres of roads. They were built to link the rest of the empire to Rome itself. To make travel as fast as possible, roads were built in straight lines taking the shortest route.

Building a road

Look

The Romans invented concrete. Look outside – can you see anything made of concrete?

Could ships sail to Rome?

Most ships were too big to sail up the river Tiber to Rome. Instead, they stopped at Rome's main port, Ostia. Here, the ship's cargo was loaded onto smaller barges and taken the final 25 kilometres to Rome.

Roman ship

Crystal ball!

The Romans often consulted a fortune-teller or a priest even before setting out on a long journey.

Did people travel in their beds?

Town streets were crowded and very dirty. Rich people travelled in curtained beds called litters, carried shoulder-high by slaves. Ordinary people used stepping-stones to avoid the mud and rubbish on the streets.

Why was Rome so beautiful?

The Romans built beautiful buildings. They invented concrete, and used clay bricks baked at high temperatures, which lasted longer than unbaked ones. Arches were built to create strong walls and doorways. Huge domes were made for buildings that were too big for wooden roofs.

Pipe up!

Our word 'plumber' comes from 'plumbum', the Latin word for the lead used by Romans to make water pipes. The same word is also used for a 'plumb-line', still in use today.

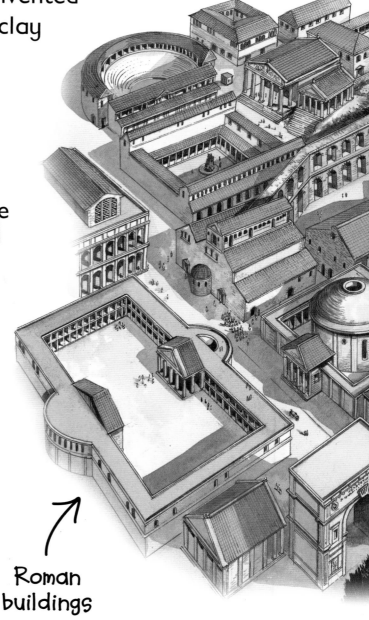

Roman buildings

Were there doctors in Rome?

Yes there were, but the Romans believed that illness was caused by witchcraft. To find a cure, they visited a temple to ask the gods to make them better. They might see a doctor who made medicines from plants or carried out simple operations.

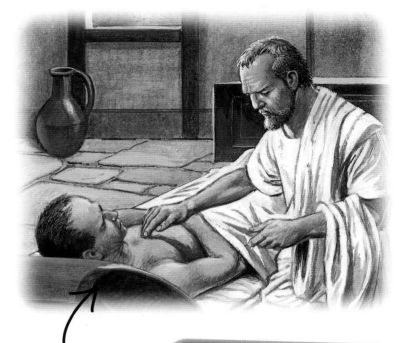

Doctor and patient

Find out

Romans spoke their own language. Can you find out what it was called?

How was Rome supplied with water?

Water from mountain springs was carried on raised stone channels into the city. Once the water reached the city, it flowed through pipes to baths, fountains and toilets.

Quiz time

Do you remember what you have read about ancient Rome? Here are some questions to test your memory. The pictures will help you. If you get stuck, read the pages again.

3. What did children learn at school?

page 8

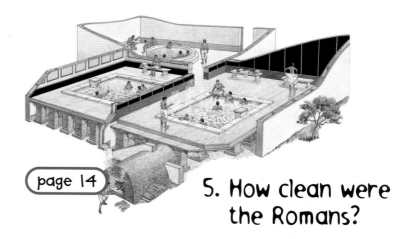

4. What was a mosaic?

page 13

page 5

1. Did people live in blocks of flats?

page 14

5. How clean were the Romans?

page 7

2. Who ate takeaways?

6. Did the Romans listen to music?

page 15

page 16

7. What was the Colosseum?

11. Who was the top god?

page 24

8. Did people keep pets?

page 21

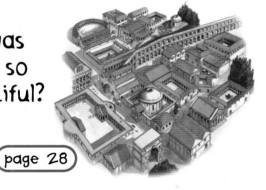

12. Did people travel in their beds?

page 27

13. Why was Rome so beautiful?

page 28

page 23

9. Why were olives so special?

10. Did grapes grow on trees?

page 23

Index

I LOVE
LUKE